9.95

DESIGN: Elements and Principles

Cliché. Oil on canvas. 56-1/4 x 42''. 1955.
Stuart Davis. The Solomon R. Guggenheim Museum.

Dorothea C. Malcolm

*Assistant Professor of Art and
Art Education*

*The William Paterson College of
New Jersey*

DESIGN:
Elements and Principles

Davis Publications, Inc.

Worcester, Massachusetts

to my best teachers, Douglas and Howard,
who always said ''let it be simply told.''

Untitled. Ink on paper mounted on cloth. 15-5/8 x 54-1/8''.
Sabro Hasegawa. The Solomon R. Guggenheim
Museum. Gift of The American Abstract Artists.

Consulting Editors:
Sarita R. Rainey and George F. Horn

Copyright 1972

Davis Publications, Inc.
Worcester, Massachusetts, U.S.A.

Library of Congress Catalog Card No.: 71-148087
ISBN 0-87192-03905
Printed in the United States of America

Printing: Davis Press, Inc.

Type: Univers Medium

Design: Panagiota Darras

Cover art: serigraph by Burton Wasserman

PREFACE

Perhaps you have observed an artist deeply in-volved in the act of creating. If you have had this experience, you might have become aware of how much the artist's personal feeling was reflected in his work.

Art, and the act of creating, is highly personal and it seems to transcend analysis. Throughout the centuries, as artists have worked in various materi-als, they have developed multitudes of design con-cepts. Some things they designed served their desires for expression better than others. Artists exchanged ideas and adapted one another's tech-niques. But it was eventually realized that beyond personal interpretation, there existed certain basic design features that appeared to be natural and common to all art.

This book contains a collection of thoughts and guidelines that are common and basic to the process of creating and to the general area referred to as design. The photographs and reproductions of works of art are intended to assist the reader in his understanding of how others have freely adapted and interpreted these basic guidelines in an attempt to successfully communicate their personal feelings and impressions.

CONTENTS

Untitled. Wall plaque clay relief. 18 x 35." 1961. Marilyn
Fox. Courtesy American Crafts Council, New York.

INTRODUCTION TO **DESIGN ELEMENTS**

Designing is relating elements, whether they are similar or contrasting, and visually arranging an interesting unity with them. Design is very much a part of our daily lives; it is found in nature as well as in our man-made environment. Design appears in many different forms and shapes and you have only to observe carefully to become aware of it. Shapes, forms, colors and textures all combine to become a unified whole which is commonly called ''a design.''

Design is everywhere. A simple example can be made with a clump of growing daisies. Each single daisy is made up of many parts. Slender, white petals surround a golden yellow center creating a contrast of bright white and yellow against a back-ground of green foliage. The petals are silken to the touch and the yellow center reminds you of the sensation of touching velvet. The whole flower is a design in itself. In combination with many other daisies, it becomes but a part of an overall design. Pleasing to the eye, although arranged at random, you become aware of shape, form, color and texture. Each individual part, unique in its own way, has carefully been placed together with all of the other parts to create a unifying and beautiful whole.

Designing, then, is the act of arranging things to create a single effect. In design, the elements are the things we work with; the principles are what we do with them. Space, line, shape, form, color, value and texture are the design elements with which artists work to create a design. The design principles of balance, movement, repetition, emphasis, contrast and unity are what artists do with the design elements to make a pleasing and satisfying art form.

Visual Dynamics. Polyethylene on wood, diagonal measurement 56 5/8 x 56-5/8". 1963. Toni Costa. Collection, The Museum of Modern Art, New York, Larry Aldrich Foundation Fund.

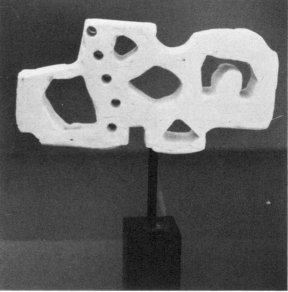

Grade 8. Wood.

8

From Within. Forged iron. 38-3/4" high. March 1953.
Eduardo Chillida. The Solomon R. Guggenheim Museum.

SPACE

Space is an element which surrounds us. It is plastic in that it stretches to infinity, can be compressed into the most minute crevice and, yet, exists only as a concept. Space can be experienced two and three dimensionally and it is a vital part of visual design. By gaining an awareness of space and the use of space in design, you will learn how it is used to express ideas. You will become aware of the importance of space in a design and learn to observe the manner in which others have used it and manipulated it to enhance their designs.

The effect of space varies with its application. An airplane seen moving across the sky is surrounded by space and a sense of openness and freedom exists. But what about the feeling of space in a crowded elevator? Space is there but the effect is entirely different.

Look around you and learn to observe space. Notice how it flows in, around, and between forms or objects.

Forms have substance and occupy space. This occupied space is known as positive space. Unoccupied, or empty space is known as negative space.

The sculptures shown here occupy positive space. The areas between and around the forms create interesting space shapes. This is called negative space. In the creation of works of art, the negative areas play a part as important to the whole design as the positive areas.

Houses. Watercolor and ink. 6-1/4" x 4-3/8". Wols. The Solomon R. Guggenheim Museum.

A flat surface has only two-dimensional space which means that it has length and width but no depth. A canvas on which an artist works is a flat surface and is called a picture plane. It is impossible to create actual depth or space on this picture plane, but an illusion of space, distance or depth is possible. Therefore, on a two-dimensional surface, space can be sensed or felt. There are many methods used by artists to create this sense of space. Many of these methods succeed in convincing the observer that there is space and depth, when, in fact, they are victims of a type of visual deception.

To your eyes, objects which move away from you appear to become smaller. As objects appear to be farther and farther away, they grow less distinct. Colors fade and blend into background colors; textures and details blend and diminish in the same manner. Although artists use these techniques to create space and depth, which represents to us the world of realism, they can also create drastically opposite effects and visual impressions.

Objects which are placed higher on a picture plane create the feeling of depth or distance. You sense that you are standing away from the objects and that there is a large amount of space in the foreground.

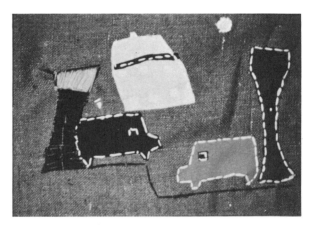

Grade 2. Appliqué.

10

Grade 8. Tempera.

Overlapping shapes tend to create a feeling of depth.

Arrangements of lights and darks can make objects appear to be solids existing in space. When light is contrasted against dark, a sense of depth is felt.

Still Life. Oil. 18 x 15-3/4''. Maurice de Vlaminck. Courtesy Greer Gallery, New York.

11

Times Square. Pen and ink on rice paper. 24-3/8 x 36-5/8''. 1955. Albert Alcalay. Collection, The Museum of Modern Art, New York.

Ten Cents a Ride. Oil on canvas. 1942. Louis Bouche. The Metropolitan Museum of Art, George A. Hearn Fund, 1942.

Depth can be suggested with the use of converging lines. Parallel lines, as they move away into the distance, appear to come closer together, thus creating the illusion of distance and depth. During the Renaissance this single idea was developed as a mechanical means to achieve this three-dimensional effect.

If in two-dimensional art space exists purely as an idea or concept, it leaves the artist free to compress or stretch it as he wishes in order to portray the particular feeling he wants. There are, indeed, many ways to deal with space in order to flatten it, keep it on the picture plane or eliminate it altogether.

Colors have an effect on space. Colors that are warm and bright often appear to be closer to the picture plane, whereas cool or dull colors tend to recede into the distance. A surface covered with colors of closely related brightness tends to blend together. As a result, the illusion of space is minimized and the space itself is condensed. When color is not used and a design is created with the use of gray tones, the closer in value that the gray tones become the more the space around the objects seems to flatten.

Oiseaux Noire Sur Fond Bistre. Oil. 16-1/2 x 21-1/4."
George Braque. Courtesy Greer Gallery, New York.

The dark bird shapes contrast sharply with the background. The effect is that of space *around* the objects.

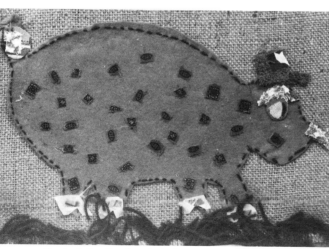

Grade 4. Appliqué and stitchery.

When the shapes and the background are closely related in tone and value, they seem to have less space between them.

Grade 1. Crayon.

Grade 5. Crayon etch.

Flat shapes can create the illusion of shallow space.

Space is reduced when a picture plane is covered with shapes which touch each other.

Outlines may be used to keep shapes closer to the picture plane.

Lucy. Oil. 30 x 18''. Wilhelm Woeller. Courtesy Greer Gallery, New York.

In this example, there is the possibility that simple shapes might have been placed on a flat surface to simply create an interesting design. Or, the shapes might have been arranged to give a feeling of dimension: the black shapes appearing to be closer than the gray mountain-like shapes.

Green Sea. Oil on canvas. 1954. Milton Avery. The Metropolitan Museum of Art, Arthur H. Hearn Fund, 1954.

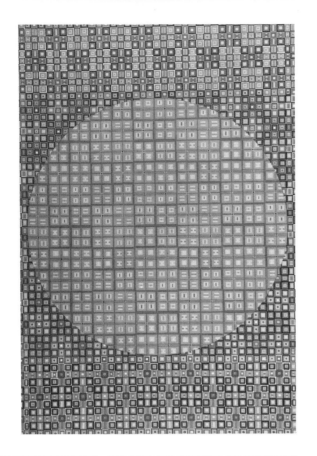

Painting A. Oil on canvas. 76-1/4 x 51-3/8''. 1961–62. Toshinobu Onosato. The Solomon R. Guggenheim Museum.

A picture plane which is covered only with patterns illustrates the ability to eliminate any feeling of space.

Shapes can appear to escape the boundaries of a picture plane.

Running White. Oil on canvas. 88 x 68''. 1959. Elllsworth Kelly. Collection, The Museum of Modern Art, New York.

Grade 4. Appliqué and stitchery.

A subjective use of space causes one to see more of what is known, rather than what can be seen from only one viewpoint. An illusion of transparency is created when the artist permits the viewer to see right through a surface. A fish is seen in an underwater environment but at the same time it is possible to see above the water.

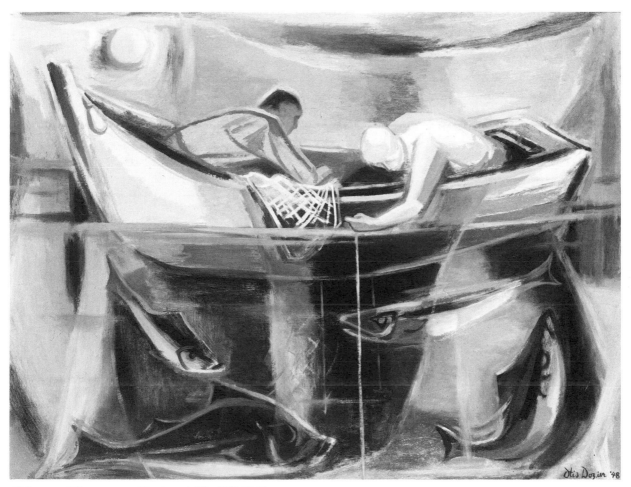

Fisherman. Oil on composition board. 28 x 36". 1948. Otis Dozier. The Metropolitan Museum of Art, Arthur H. Hearn Fund, 1951.

Grade 1. Crayon.

Space is used with great flexibility when views are combined. You are able to look directly *at* the sailor as you look *into* the boat. Notice how the train rides *on* the tracks.

It is possible to present many views. In this example the space moves and changes dramatically.

Grade 1. Crayon.

The Old House Endures. Synthetic polymer paint and collage on canvas. 47-3/8 x 47-3/8''. 1966. Michael Burt. Collection, The Museum of Modern Art, New York, Inter-American Fund.

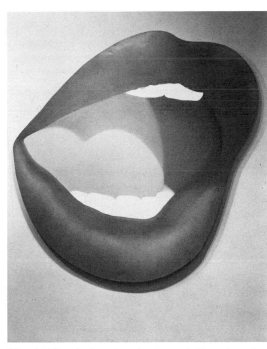

Mouth 7. Synthetic polymer paint and oil on shaped canvas. 80-1/4 x 65''. 1966. Tom Wesselman. Sidney and Harriet Janis Collection. Gift to The Museum of Modern Art, New York.

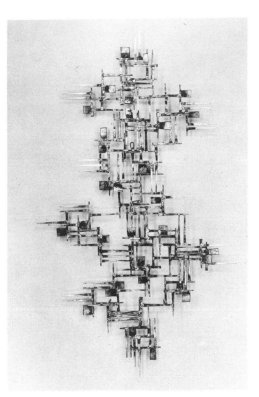

Astron. Wall sculpture. Gold-leafed steel, silver accents. 48 x 28 x 4''. William Bowie.

Grade 7. Tempera.

In the visual world, forms occupy space. Artists who create three-dimensional forms (architects, sculptors and designers) are aware that forms and space interact with each other. Because of this basic awareness they are able to shape not only the forms or objects but also the space that surrounds and penetrates the objects.

When parts or areas of a flat picture plane are physically projected *into* space, a third dimensional form is created.

Portrait. Pencil. 25-3/4 x 19-3/4". 1957. Alberto Giacometti. The Solomon R. Guggenheim Museum.

Grade 4. Oil crayon.

Slanting Red Nose. Gouache. 29-1/2 x 43-1/4". 1969. Alexander Calder. Collection, The Museum of Modern Art, New York. Gift of Mr. and Mrs. Klaus G. Perls.

Grade 2. Stitchery.

20

Line plays an important role in design. A line can simply be a mark made by a pen or drawing instrument, or it can be any continuous mark which causes your eye to follow along its path. When you rub your finger across the top of a dusty table, the mark that is left is called a line. In design, line specifically refers to an actual or an implied mark, path, mass or edge where length is dominant. Your eye readily travels along a line because a line is longer than it is wide.

A line moves, and as it does so, it indicates direction by traveling in a path that leads somewhere: up, down, under, around, through, back, forward, left, right, into, over, diagonally and across. Frequently, lines travel in many different directions at one time, creating an entirely different illusion than a single directional line.

LINE

The straight line leads the eye swiftly across the picture plane but the eye travels more slowly when following the path of the other line.

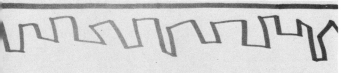

Lines appear in different ways. There are curved lines, straight lines or variations of the two. They can be long, short, thick, thin, ragged, sharp, light, dark, simple or complex. Lines can be broken and yet have direction. They can be textured and also colored.

Bold lines indicate a feeling of power.

Market, Mother and Child. Pen and ink. 9-3/4 x 20-1/2''.
Harold Altman. Collection, The Museum of Modern Art,
New York. Gift of Mr. and Mrs. Donald B. Straus.

Fine lines project a feeling of sensitivity.

Line, used in varying weights and directions with
definite control placed on its direction, can create
optical sensations.

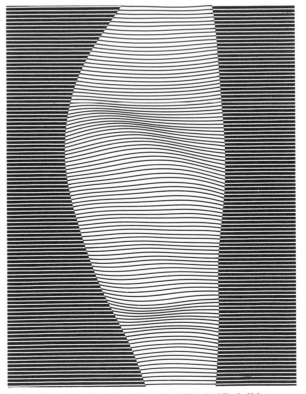

Untitled. Synthetic polymer paint on canvas. 48-1/8 x
96-1/8''. 1965. Arnold Schmidt. Collection, The Museum
of Modern Art, New York. Gift of Mr. and Mrs. Herbert C.
Bernard.

D-1-67. Pen and ink. 18-3/4 x 24-1/8''. 1967. Jeffries
Mackey. Collection, The Museum of Modern Art, New
York.

L'Homme et son Pipe. Oil. 58 x 38''. Pablo Picasso.
Courtesy Greer Gallery, New York.

Grade 6. Stitchery and appliqué.

Line is used to create accent.

A line begins, takes a path, turns and meets itself, creating a shape.

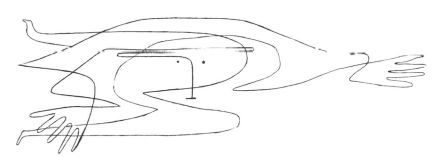

Lying As Snow, 10. Ink. 12-3/8 x 18-7/8''. 1931. Paul Klee. The Solomon R. Guggenheim Museum.

Grade 6. Stitchery.

Stitchery. Sarita Rainey.

In these drawings, each artist has demonstrated a spontaneous and sensitive use of a variety of lines.

Country House in Winter, 0. 7. Ink. 7-3/8 x 9-1/2''.
1927. Paul Klee. The Solomon R. Guggenheim Museum.

A gesture, or action drawing uses lines which attempt to show the activity of the object rather than its actual shape.

Grade 9. Ink.

A contour drawing is one in which single continuous lines follow the edges of a form.

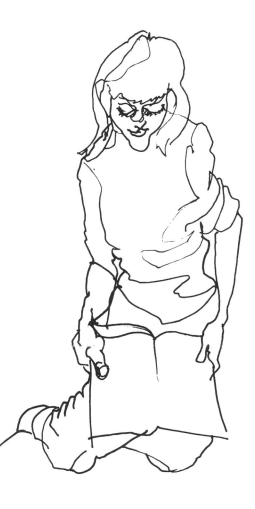

Grade 8. Ink.

Grade 10. Balsa Wood.

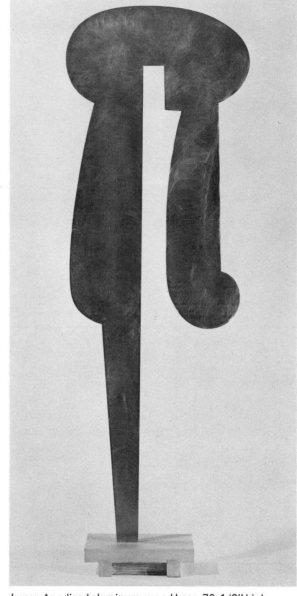

Lunar. Anodized aluminum, wood base. 70-1/2″ high. 1959–60. Isamu Noguchi. The Solomon R. Guggenheim Museum.

Although this art form is sculpture rather than drawing, its edges create visual lines which attract the eye and cause all attention to focus upon it.

26

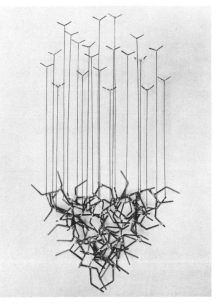

Birds in Flight. Wall sculpture. Steel with copper-coated rods, bronze accents. 37 x 21 x 4". William Bowie.

Notice how linear these forms are.

Metamorphosis-Mirror. Painted wire mesh. 31-1/4 x 23". Aluminum strip frame. 31-7/8 x 23-5/8 x 2-3/8". 1960. Manuel Rivera. The Solomon R. Guggenheim Museum.

Grade 7. Wire, wood base.

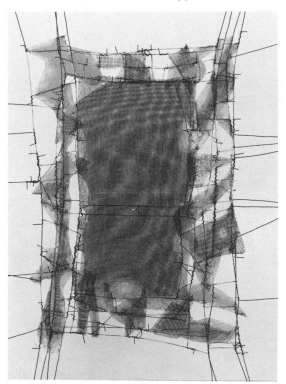

This wire sculpture presents a linear quality because the heavy wires appear to be lines in space.

You have seen how line can be used in numbers of different ways to create varying effects. Line can be expressive even when it is not representational or realistic. Look around you and notice how you are surrounded by line. Line appears in the branches of trees, in the spokes of a wheel, in the fronds of ferns and in the pencil doodling on a telephone pad.

Line is useful to artists because they can use it to quickly capture their impressions. Line, as much as space and form, is constantly around us. You will find it in the angular shapes of architecture, the flowing folds of a robe and in the curving slopes of a hillside. Do not overlook the application of line in our alphabet and numbering systems.

Dragon. Oil on canvas. 47-3/4 x 39-3/4". 1950. William Baziotes. The Metropolitan Museum of Art, Arthur H. Hearn Fund, 1950.

La Demeure Antipode. Enamel on masonite. 37-7/8 x 50-7/8". 1965. Jean Dewasne. The Solomon R. Guggenheim Museum. Gift Herbert C. Bernard, New York.

The basic geometric shapes are square, circular or triangular. Other flat geometric shapes are variations of these three.

Grade 5. Tempera and glue.

Whenever we use a line to enclose an area, we create a shape. Other ways to recognize shapes are through differences in color, value or texture between a shape and the area around it. A shape, or figure, is a positive shape and occupies positive space. The area surrounding a shape is called the background or ground. It is a negative shape and occupies negative space.

The shape of the fish is clearly distinct against the background because the line of the edge is sharply defined.

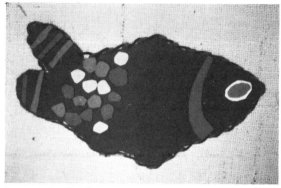

Grade 4. Appliqué.

Frequently, shapes are not clearly defined with hard, sharp edges, and it is more difficult to see where shape ends and background begins.

Grade 11. Tempera.

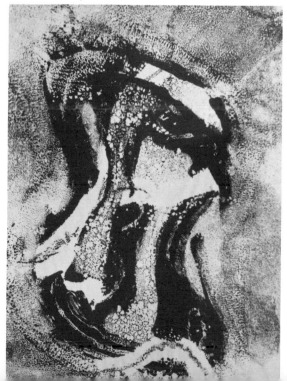

SHAPE

Grade 4. Appliqué and stitchery.

Nature provides a great variety of shapes, geometric as well as freely formed. Many shapes in nature are gently curved while others appear highly irregular. It is from these varying shapes of nature that many artists have drawn creative inspiration.

Through his imagination, the artist has invented new ways to use shape to communicate and visualize his ideas.

Grade 10. Monoprint.

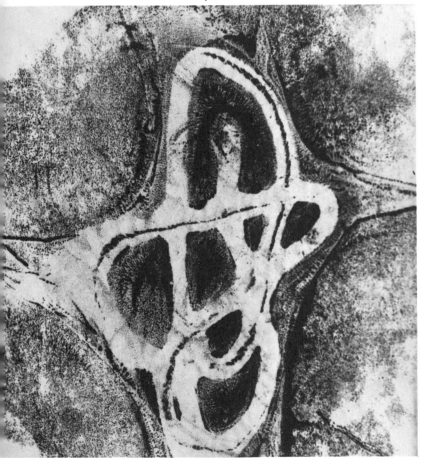

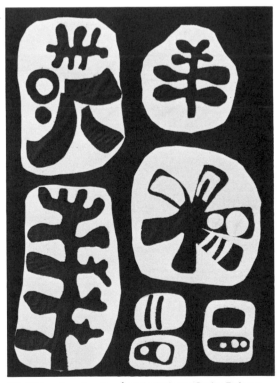

Wall Hanging. Appliqué and stitchery. Sarita Rainey.

Grade 5. Appliqué.

1, Group XI. Monoprint. 14-1/8 x 20''. c. 1948 (before)
Harry Bertoia. The Solomon R. Guggenheim Museum.

Untitled. Serigraph on paper. 24 x 19-3/4''. Henrik
Berlewi. The Solomon R. Guggenheim Museum. Gift of the
artist.

There are all kinds of shapes: solid or opaque,
linear, textured, colored and outlined. Shapes
can be transparent revealing still other shapes
behind them. Shapes might be partly covered by
other shapes, touch other shapes or stand alone.
There are shapes within shapes and shapes around
shapes. Similar shapes need not necessarily be
identical, yet they can have a common relationship
which visually ties them together. Contrasting
shapes differ from each other depending on the
treatment they have been given.

Black and White. Ink on scratchboard. 18-7/8 x 12-5/8''. 1940. I. Rice Pereira. The Solomon R. Guggenheim Museum.

Dispute. Oil. 51-1/4 x 57-1/2''. Leopold Survage. Courtesy Greer Gallery, New York.

Grade 3. Appliqué.

Some shapes will command more attention than others, depending on their size, color, value, texture, detail or their location on the picture plane.

Movement No. 2, Related to Downtown New York (*The Black Sun*). Watercolor. 21-3/4 x 26-3/4''. John Marin. The Metropolitan Museum of Art, the Alfred Stieglitz Collection, 1949.

Line and shape can be combined so that they work together to create great charm.

Grade 6. Appliqué and stitchery.

33

Grade 4. Crayon resist.

St. Severin. Oil on canvas. 44-7/8 x 35-1/8''. 1909.
Robert Delaunay. The Solomon R. Guggenheim Museum.

Shapes can promote new feelings and awaken old ones by making you relate to what is known and felt about your own environment. For example, tall shapes are elevating. Solid shapes appear to be stable. Long flat shapes express calmness; and directional, downward shapes activate the sense of falling.

34

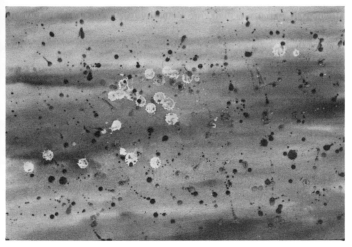

Grade 11. *Prairie Snowstorm at Sunset.* Watercolor and crayon.

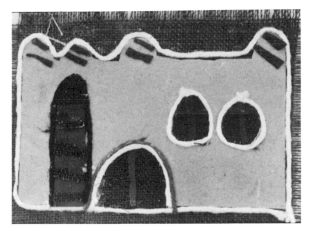

Grade 1. Felt, yarn, and burlap.

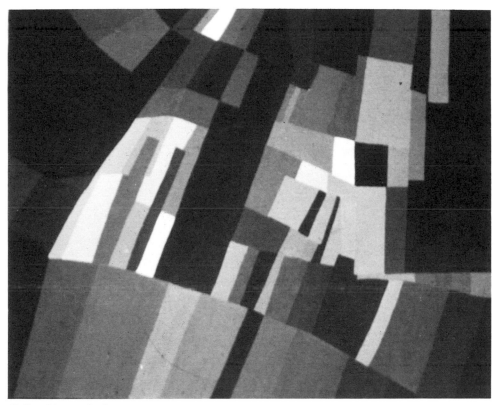

Falling Shapes. Author.

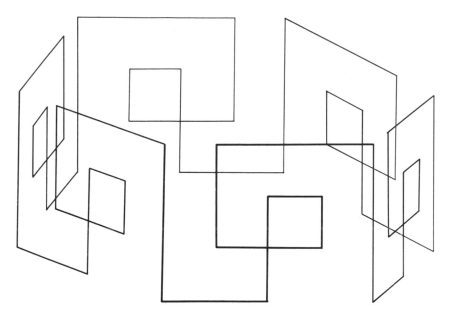

Theme Circulating Through 6 Planes, V 14. Ink. 19 x
12-1/2''. 1931. Paul Klee. The Solomon R. Guggenheim
Museum.

Planes are flat shapes. They can be joined,
separated, overlapped or can flow through one
another. These planes are geometric. They are
flowing, and are constantly moving. Some have
been created through the use of line, yet they
represent several elements of design.

MM 3. Pen and ink. 18-1/8 x 23''. 1961. Josef Albers.
Collection, The Museum of Modern Art, New York. Gift
of the artist.

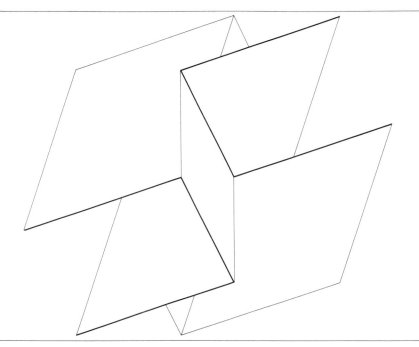

Primitive Islands. Stitchery of wool threads on natural linen ground. 1960. Evelyn Svec Ward. Courtesy Container Corporation of America, Solon, Ohio.

Notice in these pictures, the effects of the individual elements of design that have been discussed. Each one has been organized in a different manner and each has a different effect. Yet each ultimately ends in a unified and pleasing design.

Grade 7. Acrylic.

Grade 4. Tempera.

Animal and Young. Forged steel. 35'' high. November 1957. David Hayes. The Solomon R. Guggenheim Museum.

Five Red Arcs. Sheet metal, metal rods, wire. 47-1/4"
high. c. 1948. Alexander Calder. The Solomon R.
Guggenheim Musuem.

FORM

This photograph of a mobile illustrates an art form
which makes use of many different metal forms,
called planes, that glide gracefully in space.

This sculpture has many different surfaces and
surface directions, all of which are called planes.

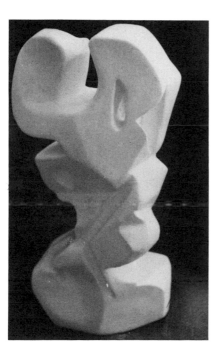

Grade 10. Artfoam.

Careful observation of the forms around you will reveal that in nature or in man-made objects, many are combinations of basic geometric forms such as spheres, cylinders, cones, cubes and pyramids.

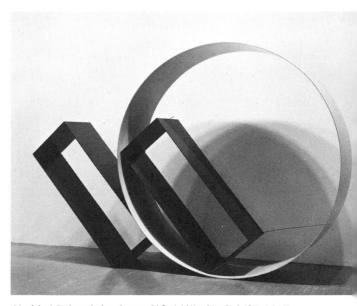

The Staircase. Wood with motor. 78-5/8'' high. 1965. Pol Bury. The Solomon R. Guggenheim Museum.

Untitled. Painted aluminum. 6' 2-1/4'' x 9' x 3-3/8''. 1967. David Annesley. Collection, The Museum of Modern Art, New York, Harry J. Rudick Fund.

Variations of geometric forms are easily recognized.

Grade 4. Paper.

College student of Sarita Rainey. Papier-mâché.

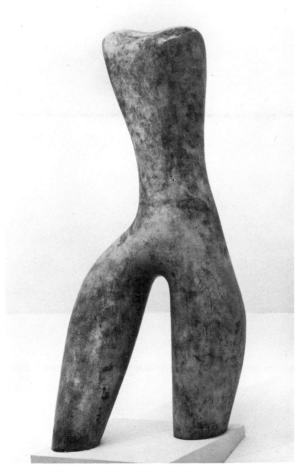

Untitled. Bronze. 56" high. 1950. Karl Hartung. The Solomon R. Guggenheim Museum. Gift of Mrs. Andrew P. Fuller, New York.

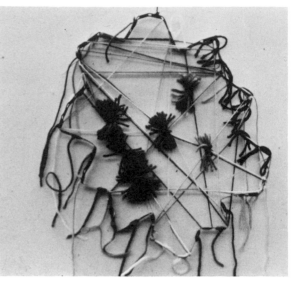

Grade 6. Wire and string.

Irregular forms are all around us too.

Wooden Horse. Natural wood. 13' high, 8' wide.
Bernard Langlais. Courtesy American Crafts Council,
New York.

This sculpture with its combination of forms and changing surfaces causes your eye to wander comfortably over and around it.

A Cloud Remembered. Ceramic. 9 x 8 x 10''; overall height, 15-7/8'', wooden base 7-1/4 x 3-5/8 x 3-5/8''. 1962. Kazuo Yagi. Collection, The Museum of Modern Art, New York, John G. Powers Fund.

There is little interaction between form and a solid mass. A solid form resists the penetration of space and is often called a closed form.

Compact Object. Assemblage: bones, thread and manufactured articles, hair, egg shell, etc. contained in polyester. 5-5/8 x 8-3/8''. 1962. Natsuyuki Nakanishi. Collection, The Museum of Modern Art, New York, Frank Crowinshield Fund.

Grade 11. Plaster.

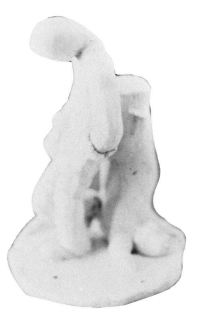

In this sculpture, space has invaded the form. This is called penetrated or open form.

Grade 7. Ceramic.

44

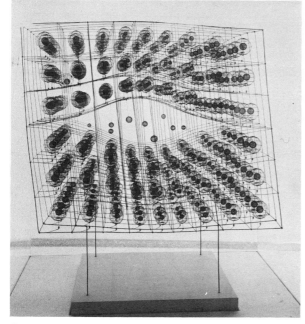

Olymp. Wire and copper balls; wooden base. 36-5/8 x 29-3/4 x 23-1/8''. 1967. Gunter Haese. The Solomon R. Guggenheim Museum.

The Nose. Bronze. 15-3/8''. 1947. Alberto Giacometti. The Solomon R. Guggenheim Museum.

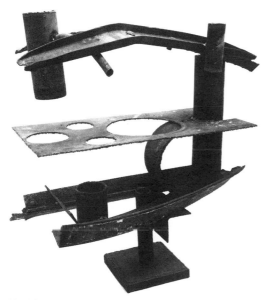

Untitled. Iron and steel. 40-1/4'' high. 1962. Richard Stankiewicz. The Solomon R. Guggenheim Museum. Gift of Mrs. Elinor L. Franklin, New York.

Space frequently dominates form.

45

Grade 7.

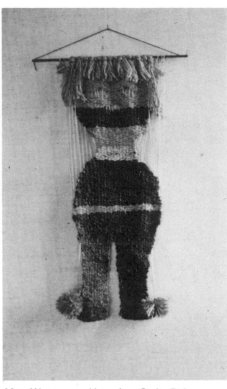

Man. Woven wool hanging. Sarita Rainey.

Grade 5. Burlap, felt, yarn, twigs.

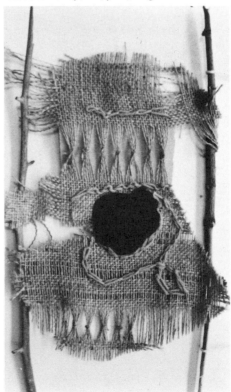

Materials differ from each other in their composition, possibility and limitation. When working with one, problems are frequently encountered which need not necessarily relate to the problems of another. In the translation of an idea from the imagination to an original art form, an artist selects a suitable material with which to work. It must satisfy and express his creative image.

As an artist works, he becomes more involved with his chosen material, and it becomes a servant to his vision. He satisfies his inner perception and often utilizes the medium in a manner other than its original purpose.

46

Big Boy. Karatsu ware. 7-7/8 x 6-7/8". 1952. Isamu Noguchi.
Collection, The Museum of Modern Art, New York,
A. Conger Goodyear Fund.

Book. Serigraph on die-cut board with linen tape spine,
10 x 10''. Pace Gallery, New York, 1968. 10 leaves. Lucas
Samaras. Collection, The Museum of Modern Art, New
York. Gift of the artist.

Color can be explained as a sensation which causes stimulation of the eye. Color attracts the eye and is one of the most obvious points of attraction around us. It has an effect which differs tremendously from person to person. The reaction to color is largely a psychological one, although there is great variety in this depending on the color and depending on the viewer. Some people react to color violently. Yet, the effect of many colors is apt to create a reaction common to most viewers. The color of a clear, bright blue sky on a cool, crisp day quickens an emotional response entirely different than a dull, overcast, gray sky. The first suggests cheerfulness; the latter invites a feeling of somberness or sadness.

Many of our associations with colors are a result of the manner in which we have been taught to think of them since we were children. How many people do you know who could easily accept a black and orange valentine? And how many people do you know who do not think that pink is for girls and blue is for boys? Color conditioning, through the centuries, has been a strong influence in man's life and in his designs. According to mythology and ancient folklore yellow, for example, has traditionally been linked with bad luck; used for bridal attire; assigned to royalty; considered a sacred color and has also warned of danger. Depending on the situation in which it is presented, man tends to accept the color and recognizes the symbolic message.

COLOR

Grade 1. Appliqué.

Color is light, and light is energy in motion. Color is represented to us through the use of pigments. They are the coloring substances that can be found in either natural or man-made things which contain color. The pigments absorb or reflect the light that surrounds them in different ways. This selective ability of the pigments in a red rose absorbs all the colors in its atmosphere, though they may be invisible to our eyes, and reflects the color red. Darkness is realized as the absence of light, and in a dark environment where there is no reflection of color, even a red rose becomes invisible. The colored inks that appear on the printed page are chemical pigments which actually reflect light and color to your eye. The amount and type of light, in combination with the brightness or whiteness of the paper all have different effects on the reflectibility of the pigments.

Hue, value and intensity are terms which are used to identify colors. Hue is the name given to a color. Value is the lightness or darkness of a color, and intensity refers to the brightness or dullness of a color. Lemon yellow, for example, is a lighter and brighter *hue* than olive green. Pink has a lighter *value* than crimson. Bright royal blue is more *intense* than powder blue.

There are various ways to change a hue, value or intensity of a color. Adding white to red changes it to a lighter red, known as a tint. A color would be darkened by adding black to it, and it could then be called a shade. Infinite variety of any color is possible depending on how much we lighten or darken it.

In art, color begins with three primary hues: red, yellow and blue. The term primary, or basic, is used because we cannot get these by mixing other colors. Primary hues occur naturally in either natural or man-made pigments. By using a range of only red, yellow and blue, we can mix many other colors. With the addition of white or black to any of the primaries, in various combinations, new colors are created; theoretically, all colors stem from the three primaries.

By mixing any two of the primary colors, a secondary color is created (orange, green, or violet). In combination, red and yellow create orange; yellow and blue create green; blue and red create violet.

An intermediate color is made by mixing a primary and a secondary color together, such as yellow-orange, blue-green, and red-violet.

The world is filled with color in many combinations of tints, shades, values and intensities. One learns to perceive color in seemingly colorless places through careful observation. Once the eye is trained to actually see, color amazingly enough makes itself known by nearly jumping out at you. There is rarely, with the exception of complete darkness, an absence of color.

A very good way to learn the effect of color and how it works is to mix them to see what happens. In just this manner, by mixing and experimenting, artists learn to use color with great sensitivity.

Grade 7. Cotton yarn.

It is generally accepted that colors are grouped into warm or cool families. Yellow reminds us of the warmth of the sun and is considered to be warm. Blue-green suggests the coolness of water and vegetation. But colors and the effects that they produce can be deceptive. Some colors may appear to be warm when placed next to a cool color. Yet the same color can be cool when placed next to a warm color.

Notice the effect of the same color when it is placed against a background of a different color.

The science relating to how we actually see color is not completely understood. Hues which are not objectively present can be created in the eyes. Be sure that you are in a good light. Gaze, but do not stare, at the green elephant until your eyes begin to tire. Then, quickly look at the blank space next to the elephant.

You should see a pink elephant. This is known as an afterimage. When our eyes become saturated with one color, they seem to demand its comple-ment, creating it if necessary. Every color has its own complement or opposite color. The comple-ment of the green elephant was the pink ele-phant. Some of the complementaries are: red and green, yellow and violet, orange and blue.

The effect of color against color becomes even more dramatic when two very intense colors are placed side by side. Each of these colors excites the eye and the visual effect is that the colors become even more brilliant. In some cases, extremely brilliant complementary colors positioned next to each other can cause an eye stimulation so great that you may have to look away for relief.

Although complementary colors can activate each other when they are seen next to each other, the same two colors mixed together to create a third can turn into a quiet neutral color. Some of the most beautiful shades of gray have come about as a result of this type of color mixing.

An artist may choose to represent an object using realistic colors.

Grade 6. Cotton woven on wire mesh.

College. Papier-mâché.

Another artist may choose to use color subjectively. He uses color to express his feelings about a subject rather than to depict it with its natural coloring.

Color, however, can stand on its own. An artist may choose to use color in a non-representational way, letting it stand alone for its own sake.

Grade 3.

56

VALUE

Between the whitest white and the blackest black
there are countless degrees of light and dark
values. Value is considered to be the lightness or
darkness of a color or of a neutral gray

The contrast in this picture is sharp and clear. In
this example, two values are noticeable: black and
light gray.

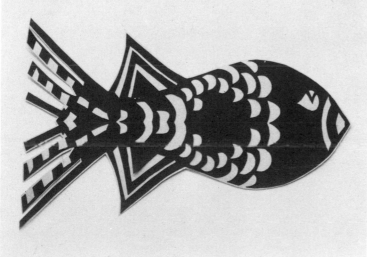

Grade 6. Paper.

Children's Party. Stitchery. Sarita Rainey.

Artists have used bold contrasts of value in order to express their feelings powerfully.

Too many values used in combination can be confusing. This application might result in a weak design. Within a limited range of values such as light, medium and dark one can find a useful variety.

Islands III. Watercolor and ink. 12-1/2 x 18-1/4''. 1933. Lyonel Feininger. The Solomon R. Guggenheim Museum.

Grade 8. Paper.

Grade 5. Crayon.

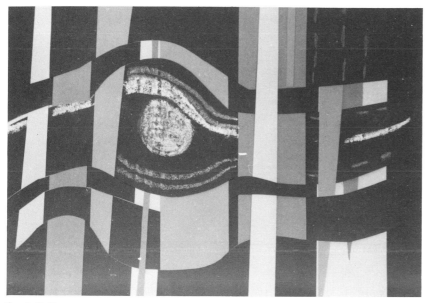

Grade 5. Paper.

Grade 6. Paint.

Each value is directly affected by the value of light or dark that surrounds it. Shapes that are close in value appear to merge together. Usually dark values appear to come forward and light values tend to recede, but the reverse can occur. Sharply contrasting values attract attention and the use of light against dark, or dark against light, can also create the illusion of size differences.

Grade 6. Stitchery.

60

Open (*B*). Oil on pressed wood. 20 x 19-5/8″. December
1940. Josef Albers. The Solomon R. Guggenheim Museum.

Value is the most elusive of all the design elements. The success or failure of a piece of work may rely on the use of the values within it. An accomplished artist has developed a sensitivity to value relationships.

Wattenmeer. Oil. 50 x 34". Wilhelm Woeller. Courtesy Greer Gallery, New York.

Grade 12. Plaster of Paris.

We are surrounded by a world of light and shadow. The brightness of a sunny day contrasts sharply with the darkness of a moonless night. The sun, traveling across the sky, creates an ever changing pattern of light and dark. Many pleasant experiences can be associated with the play of light filtering through leafy trees as the light creates moving, changing, shadow patterns.

Strong light and the presence of subtle shadow (in the partial absence of light) are artfully used in our surroundings. Architects, designers and sculptors depend on this action of light and shadow to catch and model light creating highlights, middle tones of gray values and dark values.

Grade 12. Detail plaster relief.

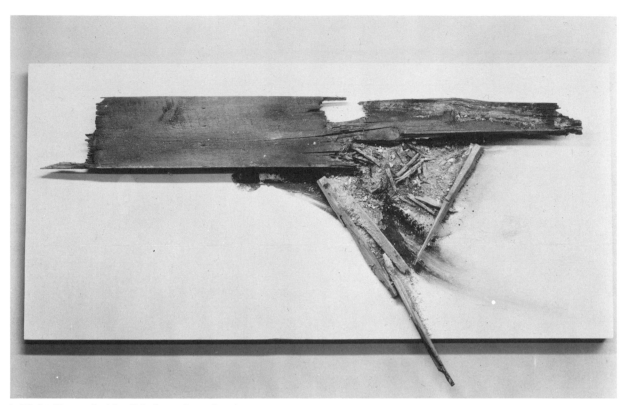

In Flight. Plywood with relief of wood, sand, polyester
resin paint. Weight, 37 lbs. 1957. Robert Mallary. Collection,
The Museum of Modern Art, New York, Larry Aldrich
Foundation Fund.

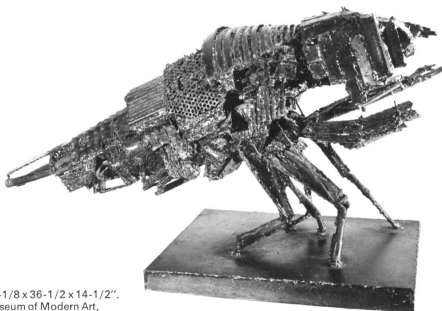

Galactic Insect. Welded iron. 19-1/8 x 36-1/2 x 14-1/2''.
1956. Cesar. Collection, The Museum of Modern Art,
New York. Gift of G. David Thompson.

64

Texture is the quality of a surface, whether it is smooth, rough, dull or glossy. We are able to observe texture, visually, through sight and the sense of touch. Pleasant or unpleasant associations are connected with this sense. The variety of reaction that is activated by touch is unlimited. Consider your own sensual reaction when you touch a feather and compare it to the sensation you feel when you touch a pineapple. Sandpaper will cause a different sensation than another texture such as the fur of a kitten.

There is a naturalness inherent in all things. Plump, soft baby skin develops into lined, aged skin of old age through a natural process of time at work. Each has attributes of its own; each belongs precisely to a particular stage of development. Artists respect this and use this knowledge to communicate their messages.

Many of us rebel against artificially embellished surfaces in order to conceal the truth of the real material beneath. We prefer to use natural surfaces and we search nature for exciting textures to use in delightful and sometimes unexpected ways.

TEXTURE

Grade 4. Bark, pine, seeds, felt, cotton yarn.

Tiger. Wood sculpture. Bernard Langlais. Courtesy American Crafts Council, New York.

65

Untitled. Woven linen wall hanging with broom corn seeds, stalks, and novelty yarns. 11 x 19''. 1963. Luella Williams. Marion Wesp, photographer. Courtesy American Crafts Council, New York.

This wall hanging uses the natural texture of seeds and reeds.

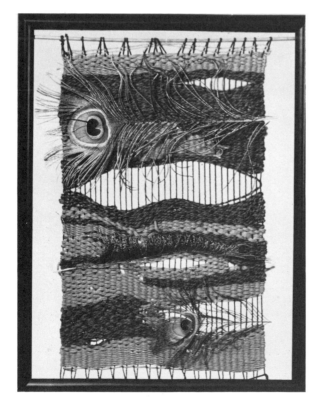

Peacock's Delight. Sarita Rainey.

"I had started this weaving while on a vacation; then came across some live peacocks. I managed to get some feathers and changed my weaving design to incorporate them."

66

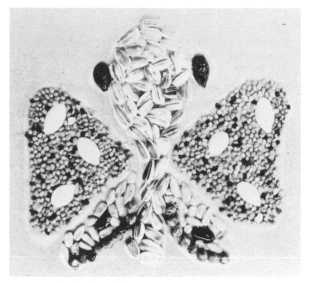

Grade 4. Corn and seeds.

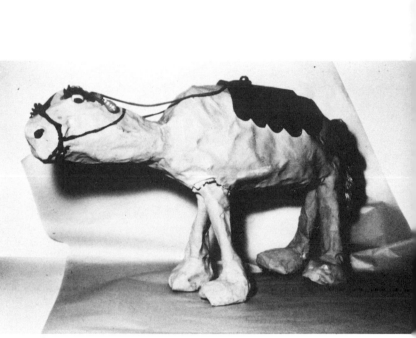

Papier-mâché. College student of Sarita Rainey.

Grade 6.

Expression is successfully reached through the use of interestingly textured man-made materials.

This collage is a combination of natural and man-made textures which promote visual and tactile pleasure.

New England Collage, II. Cedar shingles, asphalt roofing, tar paper, etc. on painted wood board. 21-1/8 x 26-5/8''. 1947. William Kienbusch. Collection, The Museum of Modern Art, New York.

Grade 5. Collage.

Assembling marvelous textures from various sources can create new and different art expressions.

Figure. Soldered iron rods with brush. 16″ high. 1959. Jim Love. Collection, The Museum of Modern Art, New York, Larry Aldrich Foundation Fund.

Poetic Object. Assemblage: stuffed parrot on wood perch, stuffed silk stocking with velvet garter, and doll's paper shoe suspended in a hollow wood frame, derby hat, hanging cork ball, celluloid fish, and engraved map. 31-7/8 x 11-7/8 x 10-1/4″. 1936. Joan Miro. Collection, The Museum of Modern Art, New York. Gift of Mr. and Mrs. Pierre Matisse.

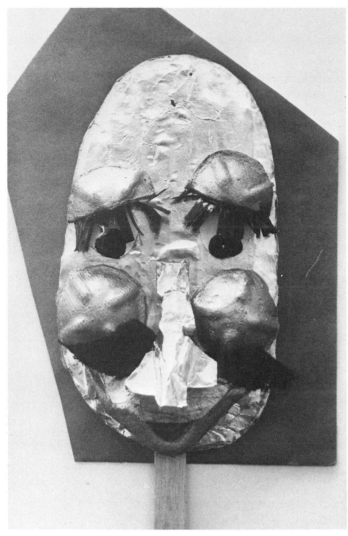

Grade 6. Cardboard covered with metallic paper.

With the use of our hands, new and interesting surfaces and textures can be created. A small, moist ball of clay can change from a smooth wet surface into nearly anything you desire. The consistency of the original material, and the sensation of the change that takes place as the clay squeezes and molds itself to conform to the pressure applied to it is an exciting experience. As compared to the monotony of the original clay ball, the finished product has a form that reflects a tremendous transformation. The eye is now able to roam in and out of it and is attracted by its new surfaces and textures. The natural response is to reach out and touch the newly formed object.

Grade 4. Yarn on burlap.

Ahab. Oil. 40 x 30″. Joachim Probst. Courtesy Greer Gallery, New York.

Oracle, No. 2. Oil and marble dust on canvas. 69-7/8 x 58-1/2″. 1962. Jack Sonenberg. The Solomon R. Guggenheim Museum. Gift, Patrick J. Lannan, New York.

Painting is not restricted to doing it in only one way. Thickly applied paint, granular substances such as sand, added to the paint, and unusually textured materials add interesting textural qualities to an otherwise traditional painting style.

71

When actual textures cannot be used, artists help us to see and feel them with our eyes. Through the artists' technique of depicting that which we know, we gain the sensation of surface or texture.

Door with Couch-grass. Oil on canvas with "assemblage." 74-3/8 x 57-1/2". October 1957. Jean Dubuffet. The Solomon R. Guggenheim Museum.

Grade 4. Oil crayon.

Texture is often referred to as ''many-ness'', because by repeating units until they blend into an acceptable pattern or whole a texture is created.

Textures can be genuine as fur, glass or thistles. Some textures are only imitations of the original and can deceive the eye through the complete similarity or likeness to the original. Part of the joy of creating is the license to invent textures through our imagination and use of materials.

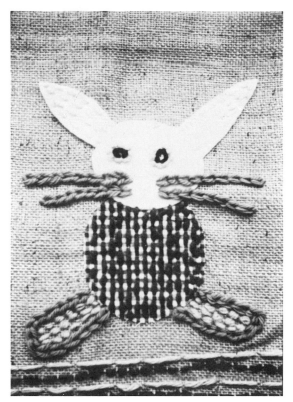

Grade 4. Yarn, felt, fabric on burlap.

Grade 5. Yarn.

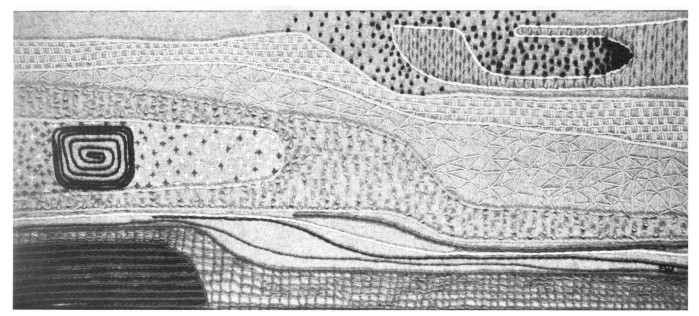

Strata. Stitchery. 33-1/2 x 14-3/4''. 1961. Evelyn Svec Ward.

73

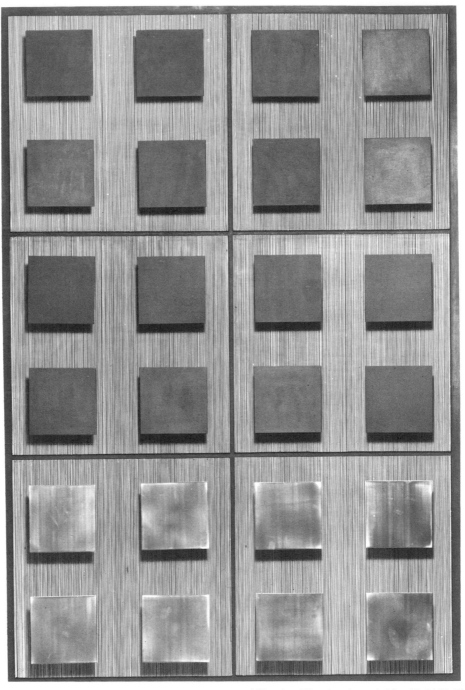

Vibration. Wood and metal. 63 x 43-1/4". 1965. Jesus Rafael Soto. The Solomon R. Guggenheim Museum.

INTRODUCTION TO **DESIGN PRINCIPLES**

Although it is not always referred to as art, everyone has the ability to translate his ideas and experiences, as well as things he sees and feels, into some form of organized, personal expression.

In every work of art there are some, or all, of the design elements: occupied and unoccupied space; varieties of line; positive and negative shape; three-dimensional form; color; value; and texture.

The manner in which these elements are used and combined determines the quality of a work of art.

In man's effort to express himself and to create meaning from the materials used, he has discovered that through thoughtfully balancing, moving, repeating, emphasizing and contrasting the design elements, he could arrive at a thoroughly satisfying and unified art form. These are known as the design principles.

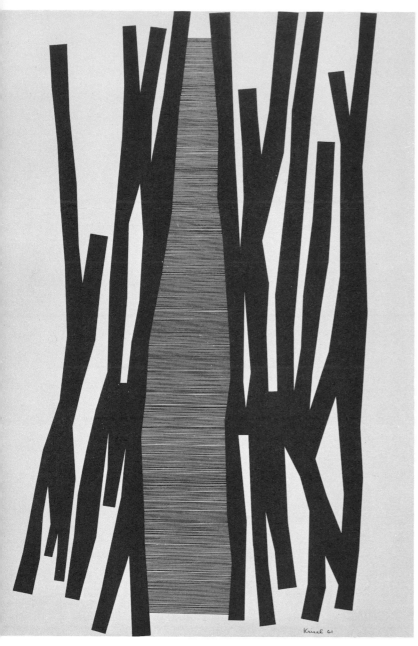

Untitled. Pen and ink. 30-1/8 x 22-1/8''. 1961. Harold
Krisel. Collection, The Museum of Modern Art, New York.

Balance is a sense of stability when applied to opposing visual attractions or forces. A tightrope walker who is slightly off balance gives a feeling of uneasiness because of our fear that he might fall. This reaction is natural because the maintenance of equilibrium is a necessary and natural function of the body.

Kindergarten. Crayon.

One naturally searches for balance around him. Balance is found more commonly in nature but it often shows up in the works of man.

In formal balance, the design elements are almost equally distributed. A design or composition which is divided in half so that one side is exactly or almost exactly the same as the other side is referred to as having symmetrical balance.

BALANCE

Grade 6. Paper.

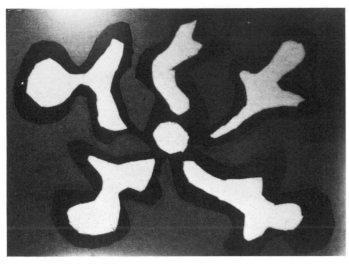

Grade 5. Felt.

Grade 4. Crayon.

In radial balance, the design elements radiate from a central point as the spokes of a wheel or in the natural form of a daisy.

Grade 5. Felt.

Grade 6. Appliqué and stitchery.

Grade 6. Appliqué.

Informal balance is asymmetrical; a center line or point is ignored and the design elements are balanced visually, though not in a symmetrical manner.

Untitled. Ink. 4-1/2 x 9-7/8''. 1957. Eduardo Chillida. The Solomon R. Guggenheim Museum.

Balance is achieved informally in dynamic designs; designs of this type are highly charged with the action of opposing forces and tensions among the elements. Usually, the larger shapes are more forceful, providing that they are closed and seem heavier than the others.

Grade 2. Crayon.

Grade 6. Appliqué.

Grade 6. Appliqué and stitchery.

Grade 6. Tempera.

The position of any particular shape in a composition contributes to its strength, too. A shape which is placed in the exact center of a picture plane is at perfect equilibrium, like being at rest. Moving the shape off center can increase its importance. A target, or bull's eye, when placed off center, attracts more attention than when placed in the exact center.

Untitled. Collage. 12-3/4 x 17-1/4''. 1956. Eduardo
Chillida. The Solomon R. Guggenheim Museum.

When a relationship exists between any two
elements, tension and opposition begin. Each
element has unique qualities and limitations and
each will affect all the other elements that come
within its influence.

This group of pictures demonstrates how each
shape affects everything else on the picture plane.

82

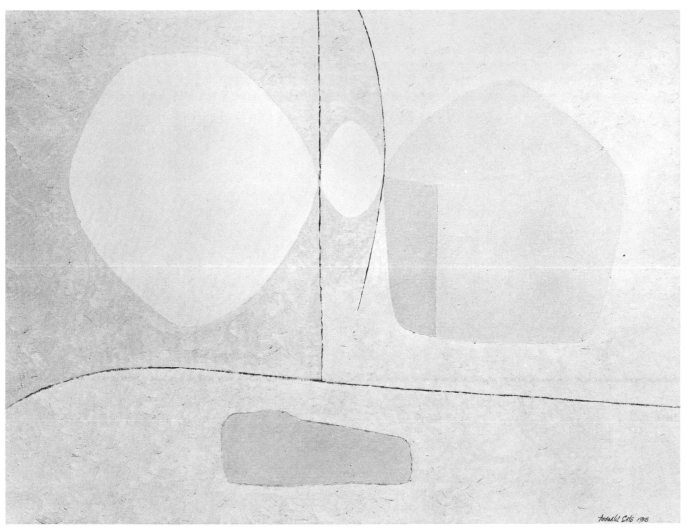

Untitled. Oil on canvas. 30-1/8 x 40.'' 1956. Tadashi Sato.
The Solomon R. Guggenheim Museum.

Grade 5. Collage.

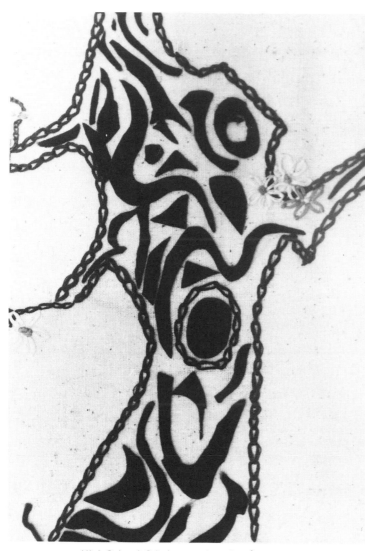

High School. Stitchery and appliqué.

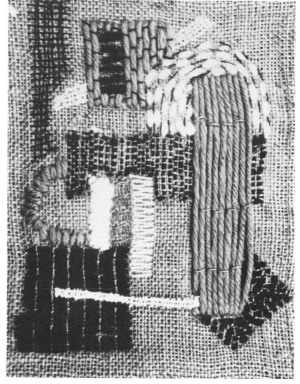

Grade 4. Stitchery.

An artist is aware of the interplay among elements
and frequently arranges and re-arranges them to
create an exciting imbalance.

84

Flowers and Shell. Watercolor. 26 x 20". Wilhelm Woeller.
Courtesy Greer Gallery, New York.

Grade 4. Oil crayon.

Often the left side and the upper part of a picture
plane attract our attention first. However, our
attention is commonly attracted and first caught
where deliberate emphasis has been placed.

Equivocation. Synthetic polymer paint on gesso panel.
26 x 26''. 1964. Benjamin Cunningham. Collection, The
Museum of Modern Art, New York, Larry Aldrich
Foundation Fund.

People, and especially artists, of the twentieth century have been deeply involved with all kinds of movement. Man has, in fact, moved off the surface of the earth into space. Artists are interested in all types of movement: moving forms, moving colors and moving patterns of light. They have created unique art forms each possessing attributes distinctly its own.

The path that our eyes follow as we look at a work of art is known as movement. By arranging the design elements an artist controls and forces this movement of our eyes and our attention is drawn to the areas of greatest interest.

MOVEMENT

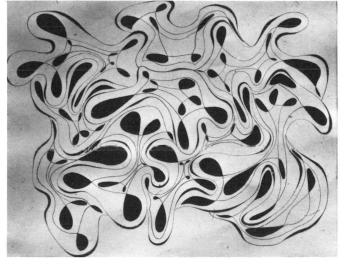

Grade 11. Tempera.

Complex arrangements have many movements and
each is planned to direct us toward a specific
point. If the artist has created a rhythmic flow,
then our eyes are easily led from one place to
another.

Family Portrait. Wood relief. 48 x 56''. Bernard Langlais.
Photographer, Peter Moore. Courtesy American Crafts
Council, New York.

Grade 7. Tempera.

Deyber. Gouache and pencil. 19-5/8 x 18-7/8". 1968.
Carlos Silva. Collection, The Museum of Modern Art,
New York.

In optical art, the movements deeply affect our
personal responses. One may experience a variety
of sensations including dizziness because our eyes
fail to focus upon one central point.

Blue and Black Construction. Tempera, paper and celluloid collage, glass, metal, wood. 20-3/4 x 14-3/4". 1936. César Domela. The Solomon R. Guggenheim Museum.

Time is associated with movement. Pictures are capable of holding our attention for varying amounts of time, either briefly or for extended periods.

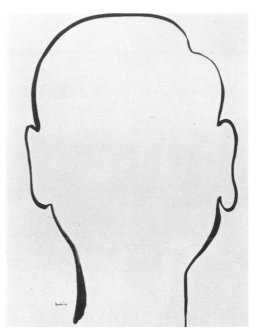

Drawing for Sculpture. Ink. 23-7/8 x 18-3/4". 1962. David Jacobs. The Solomon R. Guggenheim Museum.

Sculpture. Bronze. 22-5/8" high. 1919. Alexander Archipenko. The Solomon R. Guggenheim Museum. Gift of Katherine S. Dreier Estate.

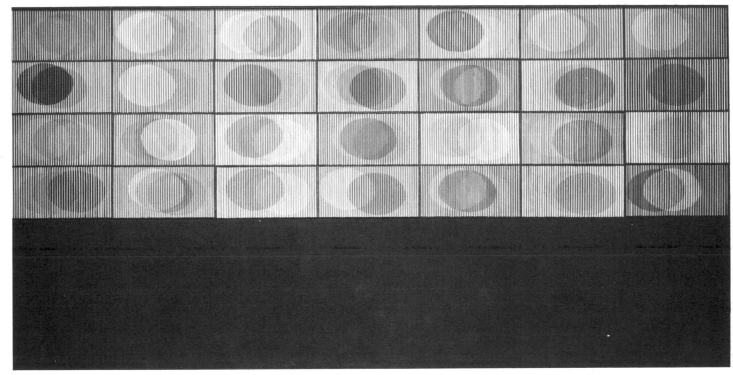

Physiochrome, 114. Synthetic polymer paint on wood
panel and on cardboard; strips of plastic strips interleaved
with projecting strips of plastic. 28 x 56-1/4". 1964.
Carlos Cruz-Diez. Collection, The Museum of Modern
Art, New York, Inter-American Fund.

A photograph cannot adequately represent this
piece of art which is so constructed that when the
viewer moves from one place to another, the design appears to move and change, too.

Pumpkins. Color woodcut. 18 x 23-7/8. 1949. Jomo-o
Inagaki. Collection The Museum of Modern Art. Gift of
Abby Aldrich Rockefeller.

Grade 5. Paper.

Repetition occurs when elements which have
something in common are repeated regularly or
irregularly, sometimes creating a rhythm. Rhythm
is a vital part of our universe and is represented in
the movement of the heavenly bodies, the seasonal
changes, the motion of ocean waves and even by
the heartbeat. Rhythm is reflected in music, dance,
poetry and visually in art.

When the interval between shapes that are exactly
alike is repeated in a uniform and regulated order,
the design tends to become more formal.

REPETITION

Untitled. 9 Steel units, 36 x 180 x 180″. 1967. Robert
Morris. The Solomon R. Guggenheim Museum.

Surface 210. Oil on canvas. 81-3/8 x 62-3/4". 1957.
Giuseppe Capogrossi. The Solomon R. Guggenheim
Museum.

By varying the length of the interval, or by changing some of the shapes while preserving the
similarity between them, a more informal interest
is created.

Flowing Phalanx. Synthetic polymer paint on canvas.
24-1/8 x 46-1/8". 1965. Francis Celentano. Collection,
The Museum of Modern Art, New York. Larry Aldrich
Foundation Fund.

Another way to maintain continuity is by increas-
ing or decreasing elements in a series: small to
large; light to dark; smooth to rough; or in the
reverse.

Seven Lithographs. Color lithograph. 19-1/2 x 25-1/2".
Alexander Calder. The Solomon R. Guggenheim Museum.

September 64. Painted metal. 16-1/8 x 88-5/8 x 48-1/4".
1964. Michael Bolus. Collection, The Museum of Modern
Art, New York.

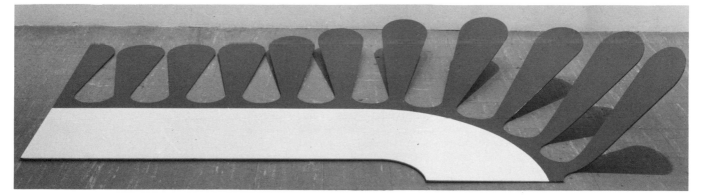

Winter Web. "Lacery Panel." 38 x 34". 1970. Evelyn Svec Ward. Courtesy Mr. and Mrs. Alan B. Kuper.

A system of repeating elements can create a rhythm or pattern. Random repeats, however, may be used without patterning. When the same color is repeated in different areas of a picture plane, its power is increased.

The repetition of some of the elements within a picture plane tends to hold the overall design together.

Grade 3. Oil crayon.

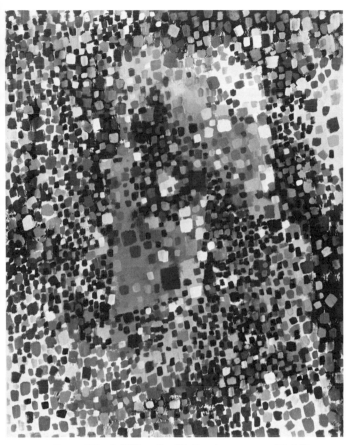

Dotted No. 2 ("New Day"). Casein on paper. 28-3/4 x
22-3/8". 1948. Robert J. Wolff. The Solomon R.
Guggenheim Museum.

Ville Jaune. Oil. 32 x 25-5/8". Leopold Survage. Courtesy
Greer Gallery, New York.

Untitled. Ink and collage. 19-7/8 x 14-3/4''. 1949. Yves
Tanguy. Solomon R. Guggenheim Museum. Gift of Kay
Sage Tanguy Estate.

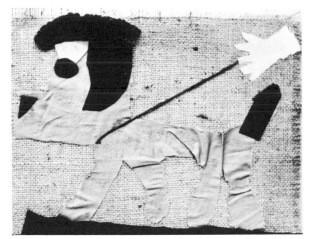

Grade 6. Collage.

Emphasis calls attention to important areas of a design and subdues everything else on the picture plane or on a three-dimensional form. By placing emphasis on certain areas of a design, an artist creates centers of interest which cause our eye to return again and again.

In a design where there are many things going on some elements may have more stress than others.

EMPHASIS

Grade 5. Printmaking.

Grade 2. Collage.

Where a linear pattern dominates a design, the attention is drawn to those lines which are larger and more prominent.

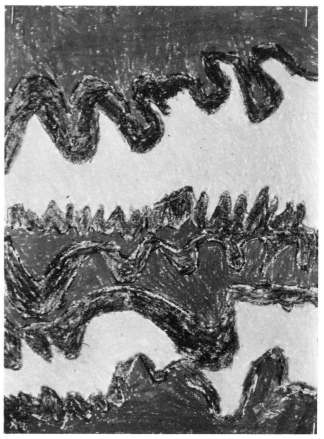

Grade 4. Oil crayon.

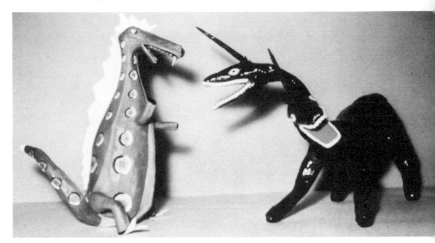

Papier-mâché. College students of Sarita Rainey.

Bold details and unusual textures, or bright colors, are more prominent than the more subdued features.

Grade 3. Stitchery.

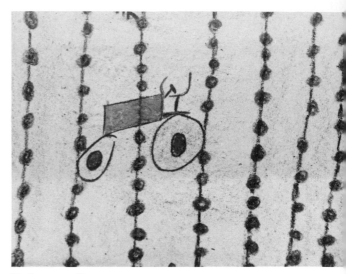

Kindergarten. Crayon.

Any one element may be positioned within the
picture plane so as to accent it and cause it to
dominate others.

Grade 7. Tempera.

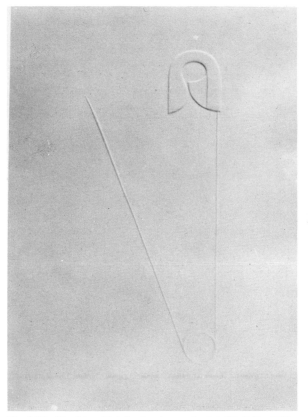

The Little Machine. Uninked embossed print. 21-3/8 x 15''. 1963. Omar Rayo. Collection, The Museum of Modern Art, New York, Inter-American Fund.

Kindergarten. Collage.

The theme or idea that the artist is attempting to portray might well be the point of emphasis.

No matter what element is chosen for emphasis, it should never demand all the attention. Emphasis is necessary but a good design is one in which all the elements work together for a unifying effect.

K. 310 (II). Acrylic on canvas. 49 x 31''. 1965–66. Leonard Brenner. The Solomon R. Guggenheim Museum.

Untitled from the portfolio "Planetary Folklore." Color
serigraph. 24-11/16 x 23-3/8". 1964. Victor de Vasarely.
Collection, The Museum of Modern Art, New York, Larry
Aldrich Fund.

Similarity of elements in a design often breeds
monotony, whereas a contrasting shape used
within the design stands out.

CONTRAST

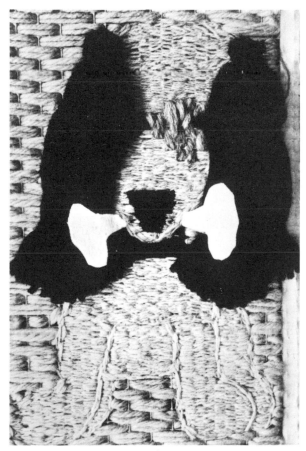

Grade 4. Stitchery and appliqué.

Elements with strong contrast stand in opposition to one another: light against dark; large against small; round against square; or smooth against rough. With consideration to color, contrast can be recognized as light colors against dark ones or warm colors contrasted against cool ones.

Work-Yellow. Oil on plywood. 71-7/8 x 71-7/8". 1958. Takeo Yamaguchi. The Solomon R. Guggenheim Museum.

Grade 5. Felt.

Grade 4. Crayon etch.

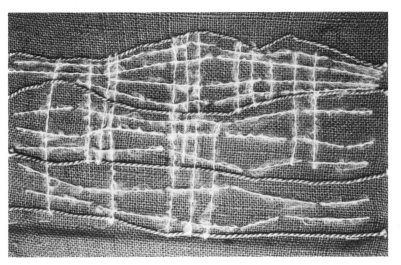

Sarita Rainey.

Contrast makes it possible to show differences and
most designs require this quality.

Contrast can be present but may be treated in a very subtle manner.

Forest. Oil on canvas. 51-1/8 x 38-1/4''. 1953. Raoul Ubac. The Solomon R. Guggenheim Museum.

Stitchery. Sarita Rainey. Collection, Mr. and Mrs. Charles Poekel.

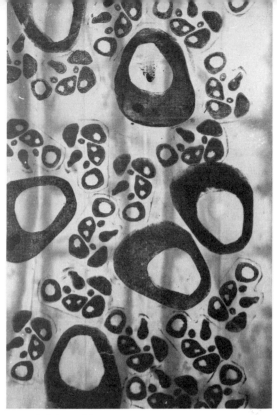

Grade 8. Printmaking.

Grade 4. Stitchery.

Grade 11. Paper.

In this group of illustrations, you can see that contrast is possible with lines, shapes, values or textures.

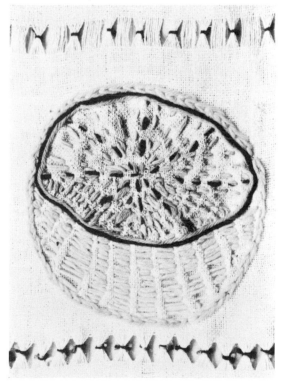

Grade 5. Appliqué and stitchery.

Frequently there will be many kinds of contrast within a single design.

One must use good judgment in dealing with contrast so that there is not too little nor too much. Otherwise, the design can become bland and uninteresting or unnecessarily confusing.

Grade 6. Pastel.

110

Grade 8. Printmaking.

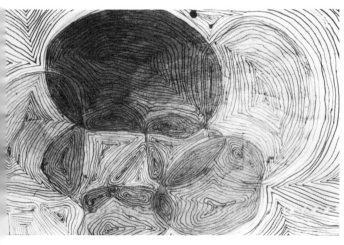

Grade 7. Tissue paper and ink.

Blind Man. Oil. 52 x 25''. New York, 1951—53. Wilhelm Woeller. Collection, Mr. Jack Palance. Courtesy Greer Gallery, New York.

Radiant Green. Synthetic polymer paint on composition
board. 16 x 16''. 1965. Richard Anuszkiewicz. Sidney
and Harriet Janis Collection. Gift to The Museum of
Modern Art, New York.

Grade 12. Wood.

Unity means oneness, consistency or integration. Unity is reached when all the elements in a design work together harmoniously. In a unified design each used element plays an important part. They all serve a particular purpose and require individual attention but they would be useless without the others.

UNITY

Grade 4. Stitchery.

Ormolu. Wall sculpture. Gold-leafed steel. 48 x 80 x 12".
William Bowie.

114

First Grade. Felt-tipped pen.

Through creative action, an artist arrives at unity by the use of imagination, reasoning and design judgments. All successful works of art reflect a certain degree of vitality, which, though it is an intangible ingredient, is a spark from the human spirit itself.

Grade 5.

Grade 11. Silk-screen.

Grade 11. Self-portrait. Charcoal.

The unity and appearance of a work of art are strongly influenced by the materials used, and all materials have particular qualities and limitations. Compare the crisp look of the silk-screened head and the delicate modeling of the self-portrait rendered in charcoal.

In addition, the manner in which the materials are handled gives each design its distinctive characteristics. Ink was used in all these drawings, but it was applied differently.

Grade 10. Pen and ink.

Grade 9. Ink and wash, wet paper.

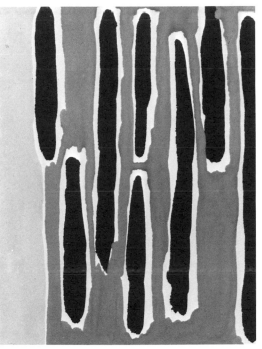

Grade 7. Ink.

Grade 8. Brushed ink, tempera background.

117

Grade 12. Charcoal.

It is the personal vision of the creator, at any given time, that makes a design different from all others. He may see a forest, but chooses to depict only a small part of the whole, perhaps, only one small tree captures his sole attention. It is possible that being in a forest arouses a mood or feeling within him which he attempts to represent rather than the way he visually sees it. There are different ways to translate this forest experience. A realistic representation on a picture plane would attempt to show us what the forest, or a selected part of the forest, looks like. But an artist may be less interested in natural appearances, and concentrates on the important characteristics of a thing. As he eliminates the superfluous, he discovers new relationships emerging among the design elements in his picture. Here is where his attention focuses. He has abstracted only what he needed from the objective world, and the less resemblance his picture has to the way things really look the more abstract his work becomes. Another artist may seek inspiration within a forest setting, yet the original stimulation cannot be identified in his picture. In fact, the arrangement of the design elements cannot be associated with any known object; this is known as non-objective art.

Grade 9. Ink.

Grade 11. Collage.

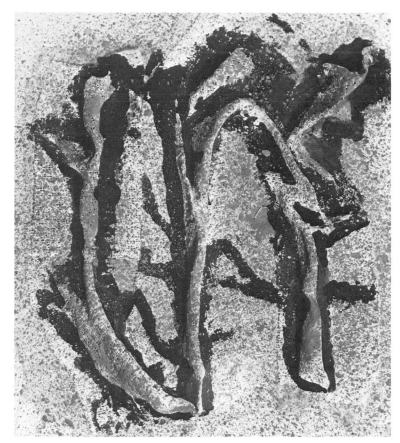

Grade 8. Pariscraft and tempera.

Rome. Acrylics. 4' x 5'. Author.

Of course, an artist does not have to call upon the objective world as a source of inspiration. He may use the vivid recall of an experience, mood or emotion. *Rome* and *A New Friend* are the personal responses of two Americans to experiences with people from other countries.

Grade 2. *A New Friend.* Crayon.

120

Untitled. Acrylics. 4′ x 6′. Author.

At times, an artist might approach his work with
no specific intentions permitting the design to
unfold as he proceeds.

Grade 11. Wire and screen.

College. Monoprint.

When an artist assembles the materials he is going to use to create an art form, he generally has some idea in mind no matter how nebulous. This mental image or idea which he endeavors to objectify sets into action his reasoning, his intuition and his skills; it demands his undivided attention. Through total involvement, each creator sets before himself a task which he alone must perform.

After an artist has willed into creation a visual work of art, it is the design elements we see arranged in some fashion. What he has done with any or all of them—space, line, shape, form, color, value and texture—determines the degree of success he has achieved.

The appreciation of good design comes with keen observation. Artists have learned to look carefully at the world around them, and respond to what they observe. Everything is subject to their scrutiny; they use every device to deepen their understanding. In addition to using their eyes in searching for the unexpected, they peer through magnifying glasses; study specimens under microscopes; and pierce surfaces through X-rays. Cross-sections of forms can reveal surprising shapes as the star in an apple, and scientific technology shows through electrical impulses diverse patterns and designs. Sensitive artists observe their world in another way, too. They respond to their environment with all their senses, and can empathize with social movements, national concerns, international problems and all conditions surrounding them. Some artists show interest in other worlds: dreams, fanciful experiences and the subconscious. All these factors can strongly influence art works.

Through acute observation and participation in art, especially in their discrete domains, painters, sculptors, architects and designers build tremendous reserves which help them in using design elements and design principles effectively. A notable difference between the artist and the non-artist is the extent of involvement in the creative process. To a greater or lesser degree anyone can learn to understand and use the design elements and the design principles for personal satisfaction and achievement.

Ecological Crisis. Acrylics. 6' x 5-3/4'.

123

Inversion. Chrome-plated steel. 29-1/4 x 49-1/2 x 29-1/2''.
1966. Eduardo Paolozzi. The Solomon R. Guggenheim
Museum.

GLOSSARY

Action drawing *See* Gesture Drawing

Asymmetrical balance *See* Informal Balance.

Center of interest An emphasized area of a design.

Closed forms Forms which resist the penetration of space.

Collage A design using natural, and man-made textures as fabrics, feathers, newspaper and string.

Color Is light.

Complementary color Every color has its own opposite color. A complementary color is an opposite color. Some of the complementary colors are: yellow and violet, red and green, blue and orange.

Contour drawing A drawing made by using single continuous lines which follow the edges of a form.

Contrast The difference between elements or the opposition to various elements.

Design The arrangement of design elements to create a single effect.

Design elements Space, line, shape, form, color, value and texture.

Design principles Balance, movement, repetition, emphasis, contrast and unity.

Emphasis Calling attention to important areas of a design.

Formal balance When a design or composition is divided in half so that one side is exactly or almost exactly the same as the other.

Gesture drawing A drawing which attempts with the use of line to show what something is doing, rather than what it is like.

Hue The name of a color: yellow, for example.

Informal balance When a center line or point is ignored and design elements are balanced asymmetrically.

Intensity Brightness or dullness of a color.

Intermediate colors Yellow-orange; yellow-green; blue-green; blue-violet; red-violet and red-orange.

Line An actual or implied mark, path, mass, or edge, where length is dominant.

Movement The path our eyes follow when we look at a design; the real movement found in some art forms.

Negative shape Background, or ground, occupying negative space.

Negative space Unoccupied, or empty space.

Open forms *See* Penetrated Forms.

Opposite colors *See* Complementary Colors.

Penetrated forms Where interaction between form and space exists in some degree.

Picture plane The flat surface on which an artist works.

Pigments The coloring substance found in all things that have color. They absorb, or reflect, the kind of light surrounding them in different ways.

Planes Flat shapes; surfaces of three-dimensional forms.

Positive shape A figure or shape occupying positive space.

Positive space Occupied space.

Primary colors Yellow, red, blue.

Radial balance When design elements radiate from a central point.

Repetition A series of repeated elements having similarity.

Secondary colors Orange, green, violet.

Shade A darkened color.

Shape An area enclosed by line, or set apart from surrounding areas by differences in color, value and/or texture.

Subjective color The use of color which reflects the way an artist feels about a subject as opposed to its natural appearance.

Symmetrical balance *See* Formal Balance.

Texture The identification of an object through the sense of touch.

Tint A lightened color.

Unity Oneness, consistency, or integration.

Value Lightness or darkness of a color; contrasts between light and dark.

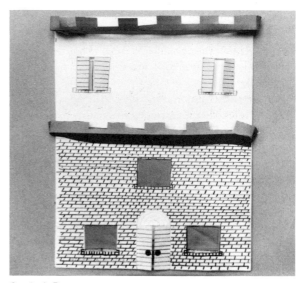

Grade 4. Paper.

126

BIBLIOGRAPHY

Albers, Josef. *Interaction of Color.* New Haven: Yale University Press, 1963.

Anderson, Donald M. *Elements of Design.* New York: Holt, Rinehart and Winston, Inc., 1961.

Arnheim, Rudolf. *Art and Visual Perception.* Berkeley: University of California Press, 1954.

Bevlin, Marjorie Elliott. *Design through Discovery.* New York: Holt, Rinehart and Winston, Inc., 1970.

Bothwell, Dorr and Marlys Frey. *Notan: the Dark-Light Principle of Design.* New York: Reinhold Book Corp., 1968.

Collier, Graham. *Form, Space and Vision: Discovering Design through Drawing.* Englewood Cliffs, New Jersey: Prentice Hall, Inc., 1963.

Cooke, Robert W. *Designing with Light . . . On Paper and Film.* Worcester, Massachusetts: Davis Publications, Inc., 1969.

Emerson, Sybil. *Design: a Creative Approach.* Scranton: International Textbook Co., 1953.

Fearing, Kelly, Evelyn Beard, and Clyde Inez Martin. *The Creative Eye,* Volume One; Volume Two. Austin, Texas: W. S. Benson and Co., 1969.

Feldman, Edmund Burke. *Art as Image and Idea.* Englewood Cliffs, New Jersey: Prentice-Hall, Inc., 1967.
    Becoming Human Through Art: Aesthetic Experience in the School. Englewood Cliffs, New Jersey: Prentice-Hall, Inc., 1970.

Garrett, Lillian. *Visual Design: a Problem-Solving Approach.* New York: Reinhold Publishing Corp., 1967.

Guyler, Vivian Varney. *Design in Nature.* Worcester, Massachusetts: Davis Publications, Inc., 1970.

Harlan, Calvin. *Vision and Invention: a Course in Art Fundamentals.* Englewood Cliffs, New Jersey: Prentice-Hall, Inc., 1970.

Hurwitz, Elizabeth Adams. *Design: a Search for Essentials.* Scranton: International Textbook Co., 1964.

Itten, Johannes. *The Art of Color: the Subjective Experience and Objective Rationale of Color.* New York: Reinhold Publishing Corp., 1961.

Kepes, Gyorgy. *Language of Vision.* Chicago: Paul Theobald and Co., 1944.

Klee, Paul. *Pedagogical Sketchbook.* New York: Nierendorf Gallery, 1944.

Kranz, Stewart, and Robert Fisher. *The Design Continuum: an Approach to Understanding Visual Forms.* New York: Reinhold Publishing Corp., 1966.

Moholy-Nagy, Lazlo. *Vision in Motion.* Chicago: Paul Theobald and Co., 1946.

Moseley, Spencer, Pauline Johnson, and Hazel Koenig. *Crafts Design: an Illustrated Guide.* Belmont, California: Wadsworth Publishing Co., Inc., 1962.

Ocvirk, Otto G., Robert Bone, Robert Stinson, and Philip Wigg. *Art Fundamentals: Theory and Practice.* Dubuque, Iowa: Wm. C. Brown Co., Publishers, 1962.

Oster, Gerald. *The Science of Moiré Patterns.* Barrington, New Jersey: Edmund Scientific Co., 1965.

Randall, Reino and Edward C. Haines. *Design in Three Dimensions.* Worcester, Massachusetts: Davis Publications, Inc., 1965.

Sausmarez, Maurice de. *Basic Design: the Dynamics of Visual Form.* New York: Reinhold Publishing Corp., 1964.

Schinneller, James A. *Art: Search and Self Discovery.* Scranton: International Textbook Co., 1961.

Wilson, Robert C. *An Alphabet of Visual Experience.* Scranton: International Textbook Co., 1966.

ACKNOWLEDGMENTS

This book would not have been possible had I not received the gracious cooperation of artists, craftsmen, museums, galleries, private collectors, and agencies. It was a pleasure, indeed, to work with them; and I am grateful for all their help.

I want to extend my sincere appreciation to Sarita Rainey, Supervisor of Art, Montclair Public Schools, Montclair, New Jersey, and her students who contributed much of the student artwork in the book. My thanks also go to Gretchen Sanderson; Betty Hardy of Pennsylvania; Margaret Buckley of the Hawthorne School in Teaneck, New Jersey, J. E. Flood and L. La Iacona of the Park Ridge, New Jersey, High School; and all their students whose works appear in the book. Thanks are extended to the students represented from my own collection which covers a period of years.

I am grateful for the help these people gave me; each in his own way: Manual Greer—the Greer Gallery, New York; Gene Derr—The Sculpture Studio, Inc., New York; Richard Bittenbinder—the Container Corporation of America, Solon, Ohio; George Horn—Baltimore Public Schools, Baltimore, Maryland; Barbara Elson and Elizabeth Simons of New Jersey; Cheryl McClenney, Agnes Schipper, Esther Carpenter, Linda Loving, and Nada Saporiti of New York; my family, colleagues, and friends who offered suggestions and gave encouragement.

Figure. Bronze. 16″ high. 1958. Philippe Hiquily. The Solomon R. Guggenheim Museum.

128